Surviving the Moment of Impact

T. Cole Rachel

Soft Skull Press
2002

surviving the moment of impact
isbn:1-887128-86-7
©2002 by T. Cole Rachel

First Edition

Acknowledgements
The following poems have appeared elsewhere prior to this collection:
  "ties" — *The Ontario Review*
  "my father, one of those things i never write about" received the T. Marsh Reese
    prize from the Academy of American Poets, and *The Ontario Review*
  "the project of the poem" — *The Ontario Review*
  "elegy for a cousin who has fallen off the face of the planet" — *The Ontario Review*
  "six degrees of the devil" — *Sierra Nevada College Review*
  "retained" — *Sierra Nevada College Review*
  "cadaver poem" — *Illuminations*
  "saved from drowning" — *Owen Wister Review*
  "what is left" — *Mikrokosmos*
  "things that are lost" — *Ellipsis: Literature and Art*
  "suspension of disbelief" — *Westview*
  "the grandparents" — *Westview*

cover design: Claudia Michael Brown
author photographs: Ignacio Mardones
book design: David Janik
editorial: Tennessee Jones

distributed by
Publishers Group West
1.800.788.3123
www.pgw.com

Soft Skull Press
107 Norfolk Street
New York, NY 10002
www.softskull.com

Thank you to those who have helped save my poetry and my sanity: to friends both close by and far away, particularly Albert Goldbarth, Rita Costello and Jeanine Hathaway, whose kindness and thoughtful input have been a blessing to me, to Bret Easton Ellis, Edmund White, Michael Carroll and Ignacio Mardones, without whom neither I nor this book would now exist; and to my family, whose support, courage and amazing lives have made these poems possible.

table of contents

I. myths: living and dead

II. taking your life in your own hands

III. what happens now

Miles, etc.

It's old news now, that a good poem is the end-point of some journey undertaken—or many. I'm thinking, for instance, of Chaucer's pilgrims and Coleridge's Mariner, as well as the psychological light-years zapped across Dickinson's brain while she sat in place in Amherst, Massachusetts.

This is old news that, in the right hands, still feels current; and it's a pleasure to experience the vastness travelled in Cole Rachel's poems, from a childhood in the rough sun-hammered, psyche-stunting trailer world of Hydro, Oklahoma, to an adult life of empathy and wry humor that can look back with a wonderful blend of the tender and of the aghast; the urbane and the playful; the forgiving and the rancorous; the silly and the dead-sober introspective.

I may not be completely objective in this: I directed Cole's MFA thesis. But I've shared these poems with enough good readers—strangers to Cole—to see that the work's delights are indeed built into its words.

And I may be misleading and narrow if I've led you to believe these poems are nothing but autobiography; in substance and in form, there's a flexibility here that steps outside the limits of confession. Still if "journeying" is my organizational metaphor, these poems do appear to be earned by the miles an actual life has travelled—and not just in the sense of Oklahoma to New York City, but also in the sense of a speaker who seems to have "gone the distance" as measured in units of mind and heart.

I've long admired the final line of the final poem of this book—in a way, it ought to be the title for *all* books of poetry—but DON'T turn straight to it now. (I *said* DON'T.) Earn it, by making the journey, the way these poems and their author have.

Buckle up.

Albert Goldbarth
August 2001

I. myths: living and dead

*The perplexing thing is that the best and worst of times for me—
when I felt that I was living full-out with real ferocity, but also
suffering from a crisis of hopelessness—were almost simultane-
ous. I was wildly alive and nearly dead at the very same time.*
                    —Rick Whitaker, *Assuming the Position*

Our lives are at once mythical and ordinary.
                    —Natalie Goldberg, *Writing Down the Bones*

mcpoem

(start with a hook)

> it is summer when we fuck
> so she crawled under the house and died
> they're much easier to deal with this way, mummified
> people should know when they are trying to kill you
> sometimes it happens like this

(supply a narrative)

> i walked on ice, thin as peanut brittle
> on summer nights we slept on air mattresses that smelled
> and i lie in what has become my sister's bedroom—horses
> the vents blow sweet cold death into every room
> you tell it like an after-school special

(stop on a moment)

> your eyes suddenly beestung with the telling of it
> i realize this at some point in the am, hiding
> and found textures becoming a bullwhip
> but the cat stops me, creeping
> and you hear it and suddenly know

(establish closure)

> needing to look up through the branches, not knowing
> that for years i would feel it on me, wash
> grateful to have been pulled
> silently biding their time
> at how beautiful we can become

(end with a line of irony)

july 4, 1996

on the fourth of july i see my mother
illuminated by the strobe-flash, sparkle
spray of cheap fireworks, in our yard
with her hair pulled back, she hold the fire
setting off class D cardboard explosions
with the tip of her cigarette

her face half-hidden by smoke and
night, i think that she is nothing at all
like those childhood photographs that
hang in my grandmother's spare bedroom
she does not fade
she does not force a smile
she does not curl
against the glass

sitting on the front porch, i am
the good son, again, watching that older
female version of myself walk barefoot
across the burnt grass, the wheat
fields stretch out around us and my
mother launches plastic rockets that drop
delicate tissue parachutes,
flickering and dying out like a lifetime
of summer holidays all shot in one moment
i close my eyes and smell the 4th of july,
tugging at my thrift store sleeve

before leaving

the nurse has painted your fingernails
an almost radiant raspberry, a color reminiscent
of those tiny flowers that you used to grow
on the back porch, back when i was small
and you made me lunch and gave me
eskimo pies

you seemed ancient even then, your cane
leaving black smudges on the kitchen linoleum
you watched from the window
as i circled your house on bicycle
it was as if you had no age, only years
of quilt blocks and yellow newspapers,
a house filled with old things

i try to imagine you the way you were before
your fingers not yet the claws of age, curled
from years of solitary gardening and
the worried clenching of someone left
to live alone

i wonder what you must have been like
before you became the withered widow-woman
who over the years descended
like an arthritic bird
into a brown recliner
covered with quilts

i want to tell you that you are too good
for this world, that age has treated you unfairly
i want to tell you that you are gentle and
wonderful, but i don't
i tell you that i miss you
i count the pill bottles on the coffee table
i notice the way the grips on your walker
have worn thin from years of use
i tell you that your nails are pretty

pulled

they have pulled all of her teeth, 17
at once while i sit, numbed by a stack
of national geographics older than me

i wonder if she might want to keep them, strung
on a tribal necklace, each of them symbolic
of battle, years of chewed food and tragedy
little gnarled dental reminders of the words
spat out before the teeth turned dark
and decided to break

that night she is sick on the couch and
i assume my rightful place on the floor
she curses them, hateful plastic, devil
dentures. i imagine them flying out in
the night, chattering across the floor at me
exorcist teeth

this is nothing new, this knowing
that i am her, this certainty
that i should get up and make this right
place 17 dollar bills under her head, leave
the house while everything is still ok

but the cat stops me, creeping
through the room with white mewling baby
clutched in her mouth, limp
and a look that sends me back

to the waiting room, white walls
and the soothing, practiced voice
of the dentist
        it's almost over now
        once these things have been pulled
        there's no putting them back in

winners never quit

and quitters never win, he'd say, dispensing it with the same tone
used to deliver lectures, sermons
and endless amounts of downhome sloganeering
everything repeated twice for emphasis

oh, i gau-ran-tee it. winners never quit, they just keep on
keepin' on. just think about those hobos riding the rails, looking for work
sleeping in their shoes. destitutes and no accounts, winos mostly
but they keep on trying. they wake up and they try—just like us.
trying even when you always fail—now that's winning.

and I can't help but imagine them like the sad figurines haunting
my aunt's dining room—
these hobos crowded into boxcars, the bright patches on their jackets
shining in the darkness, greasepaint frowns painted
on their scruffy faces, the deafening sound of spoons rattling around
in their tin pork and bean cans, all of them careful
not to poke each other in the eye
with their crooked tree branches, on which polka-dotted handkerchiefs carry
all their worldly possessions. these were the men i thought of when he talked
about success and failure, these bums and transients. winners.

for years i would think of it this way—all of us destitute, rejected
circus clowns, living in the honest dignity of repeated defeat.
i'd think of him with his used car lot and endless junk collection, the rest of us
scratching in the dirt, everyone desperately winning.

where he's been

the house was destroyed when we got there
front door knocked from its hinges, revealing
an interior littered with broken glass and upended
brown vinyl couches, the disturbing remains
of potted plants

we walked through it without speaking
my mother cursing under her breath, exploring
the chaotic muddle that had once been familiar,
safe. the brass bed on its side, still perfectly made
the walls naked except for fist-sized holes,
empty black sockets

next we are on the uneven sidewalk, surrounded
by stripped trees, leaves snapping underfoot
like the bones of small animals. my mother speaks
saying words that must seem as vital and necessary
as lungs or blood
everything is going to be ok.
i'm ok.
but spoken they become stones, undigestible
hard spots thrown at me for comfort
and i listen instead to the dead air in the phone receiver
still caught in my glove, snapped cord trailing out behind
connected to nothing

they speak adult in my grandmother's kitchen
bouncing words off the cigarette smoke
and warped linoleum floors, sure
that none of them will land on me and stick
unaware that it's already too late
i know where my father has been

the wait

i used to sneak out of the house to do it
when i was small
during the winter
i walked past the remains of the garden,
vines crumbling to dust on a barbed-wire fence
crawling under electric wire that held in
no cows and one lethargic and mean-spirited
shetland pony

i walked down transparent dirt paths
through coarse weeds and thorn bushes
oblivious to any season
i climbed down embankments of red dirt
held together by explosions of dead tree roots
all this to walk on ice, thin layers of it
covering barely existent ponds hidden in baby canyons
behind our house

i walked on ice, thin as peanut brittle
a membrane between myself and
black, trash-filled creekwater

cars would pass on 66 bridge somewhere above me
as i slowly worked my way towards the middle
ice creaking and moaning underfoot like a rusty hinge,
becoming in spots like frosted glass, revealing shifting
air bubbles beneath

sometimes i would pause, standing still and ghost-quiet
but never for long
i moved always
towards dead center
where i knew the ice was the thinnest
the spot where physics would give way to oblivion
leaving me in the hands of hateful gravity,
eager to pull me under

always for that moment
alone in the center of the ice
counting slow seconds under my breath
waiting for the moment that my whole life told me
would inevitably come

it catches up with me
to this day
alone, i find myself at the thinnest spot
where almost nothing separates me
from a coldness that would consume everything

the proof

i kept them for myself, pulled them
from the wreckage of shoeboxes and overstuffed
junk drawers, stockpiling the white paper wal-mart
envelopes in which they were separated—
pushed to the back like weaklings
in a photographic gym class

i hoarded these celluloid bills like currency
coating the double-paned windows of our trailer
with tape and negative, choosing
to view the hostage moments as smaller
easily rearranged cells, divided
brown purple plastic artifacts
revealing us as alien, thumbprinting
our insides, decoding forced smiles
as violet grey smears of grimace
exposing midwestern mannequin parents
as victims rather than unwitting executioners
the boy as a tow head baby monster
held down by a party hat, biding his time
until he can devour the others for lack
of understanding

eventually everything becomes this—
reversed, grey, foreign
not yet once-removed from reality
by kodachrome paper and lying
chemical color processing. better
seen through these bits of holy
plastic, objects touched by the light
of that moment. evidence
we can be nothing that we appear

"yr so great"

a week before the party we decorate our valentine
sacks, the classroom suddenly a sweatshop
of heart-cutting and uneasy elmers glue application
resulting in classroom walls lined with sweetness, explosions of glitter
with open, love-starved mouths

when the day comes, we are a tornado of psychotic energy—
scattering the room with cupcakes, candy hearts
the consistency of chalk, spilled orange drink
slicking the floors as we deposit our miniature cards,
one in each bag—everybody loving everybody
even if you hate them

so in the melee of mail delivery, i slip
an extra valentine into jeremy squires gift bag, a poorly adorned
thing revealing only his name and a hot pink machine gun, an image
that does nothing but increase my suffocating affection for him.
i breathe deeply and make my deposit, unnoticed
leaving behind my own special edition—
a thing born of cardboard and scotch tape that has lived
with me for weeks prior, emanating
an imagined heat through the thick canvas of my charlie brown backpack

he will read this and he will know   i imagine
our eyes meeting across a crowded classroom, a silent recognition
that no ice cream cone cupcakes could disturb.
we are soulmates   we are meant to be together
this will be our own special secret
and at my own neat desk, neatly dividing my own valentines
by size and color, the imminent forging of our psychic connection
makes me silently terrified

"YR SO GREAT . . . who wrote this?"
his voice, and i pretend not to hear, rifling
through my candy and tiny white envelopes.
"let me see that" says the black-headed girl
who i will hate from this day forward, "oh, he wrote it"
and heads turn in my direction, cupcakes pause
"cuz he's the only boy i know who writes this much
like a girl."

and here selective deafness ensues, i ogle my candy
clutching jeremy's own generically scrawled valentine
under my desk, remembering to be smart and keep quiet,
reminding myself to stay away from those boys
who make me too happy.
all the while my left hand practices, repeatedly
and with careful deliberation,
to undo the neatness of my name

the things that wait

they hung in her closet for months after she died
obscene reds and assorted shades of blue, defiantly holding on
to that old lady smell—a fragrance captured and reproduced by avon
in a million not-so-subtle hues, held in amber-tinted cologne
that would sit for years on shelves in my grandmother's bathroom
above a toilet wearing fuzzy pink lid-covers, hidden
in elaborately shaped glass bottles
a porcelain poodle
the crystal liberty bell
cinderella's glass slipper

i was required to search the pockets of her pant suits, removing wads of tissue
used to perhaps discreetly blow her nose in church or to dab the corners
of eyes clouded by cataracts and moved daily to tears
by the bold and the beautiful
i'm amazed at the sight of them—garish and unwrinkled, synthetic
and timeless as atom bombs
i stuff them into asphalt-colored biodegradable bags and wonder
at what point did these pants take over?
at what point were her dresses and broomstick
skirts replaced with these—formless
uniforms made to withstand stains and taste and time?

as i heft bags of her clothes through the doors of the disabled american veterans
thrift store, i am confronted again
by my own geriatric phobia
not in the forms of the shuffling arthritic walker-pushers
or stained hospital beds
but by a tickling anxiety
solidified into a rainbow of elastic-
waisted slacks, scarier
than alzheimers or my great-grandfather's
emphysema, rows and rows
of endless polyester, pulled
from the closets of dead grandparents
choking the aisles with the lonely smell
of bingo halls and social security
silently biding their time
on metal hangers

things that are lost

i sat on top of a refrigerator for hours
alongside a wooden crate housing
dog food and bird seed, watching the camel humps
of 66 highway with binoculars, scanning
for the mail truck or the prehistoric lump of my grandmother's
mercury cougar, which delivered her on weekends
heavy with milky way bars and kentucky fried chicken

and this vigil brought with it always the same fantasy, forgotten
and reborn week after week in dirt and binocular sweat and hills
pocked with pumping oil wells—
a ghost version of me walks the bent-finger of road to our mailbox
removes propane bills and reader's digests
continues the curve of road, never looks to the house
and never returns

my fingers pick up the binoculars, focusing
on the farthest horizon, a flash of deer-crossing sign
suddenly a glimpse of my blonde bowl cut, a fencepost my skinny spectral legs
heading into shimmery highway with a pocket of phone bills and junk mail
i wave goodbye to myself, off to devour a life no trailer, no rock canyons,
no rabbit hutches or rope swings could hold

later when sleep doesn't happen or rain falls against glass,
i get out of bed and look past whatever is there
hoping to be haunted by a short piece of gravel road, a gangly
pencil-stick shadow stretched across red dirt,
the approach of a thing that has lived, the measured steps
of someone who has practiced escape

removing the dead

so she crawled under the house and died
and less than a week later, after failed barn-searchings
and pasture-sweeps, the vents blow sweet
cold death into every room of the trailer
and we know

she stays, a rotten air that lives
like an extra person in the house, fond
of closets and lingering in the kitchen

it makes you wild
with incense and open windows, lysol
in the floor vents, and all of us sitting
out in blistering heat to avoid the evidence

        it's even worse than cigarette smoke
and you light one on the burner of the stove
it will be weeks before you stop obsessively washing
your hair, burning vanilla candles

so when the stench becomes so violent
that we could no longer eat, we are forced
outside, tugging back trailer trim, the tin skirt
a stubborn band-aid finally pulling free

she looks to be sleeping, curled in the lunar
dirt under the bathroom, a fur halo blowing
back from the skull, body matted into the earth
waiting patiently to be extricated with the rusty
end of a garden rake

we are quiet in the presence of what's left
you stand back, stilled
not by a wave of decay, rolling out like heat
from a furnace
not by the black empty eye holes
or the delicate curvature of exposed
tail bones, but by naked forearms
mine, which i've forgotten to hide
coated with roadmaps of red wound
a million tiny razor slashes, fiery and meticulous
as my handwriting
not knowing this has already been a death house,
not knowing that for years i would feel it on me, wash
my hands of it daily, and every summer wear long sleeves
you say, once
       go back inside

II. taking your life in your own hands

Poems, despite their obscurity, tend to be attempts at clarifications.
—Charles Simic, *The Poet's Notebook*

So just maybe *it is these small silent moments which are the true story-making events of our lives.*
—Douglas Coupland, *Life After God*

the poem is

not always your friend, it is not
the roomie who holds back your hair
as you vomit your insides onto white
notebook paper, it prefers
to hold your head down
in the toilet that is your life
and flush repeatedly

it makes you tell the truth, possibly
wringing out horrible things
about your family
it mocks you
with the artifice of love
it exposes with deadly accuracy
the nature of your frailty
it climbs to places just out of reach, saying
      you are not good enough to write me
      you are a coward

and then, when you think this poem
has gone, it raises the blinds
and wakes you, begging
shut up and look, you idiot
      look, just for a moment
      at how beautiful we can become

surviving the moment of impact

it's like restaging a play, equal parts
rudnick and euripides, the protagonist
somewhere children grow up to be normal
returns to his childhood home, all wood paneling
and farm implements, and is confronted, literally, figuratively
somewhere people pay bills and don't lose sleep over paying for
school pictures, 3 dollar lunches, antibiotics
by the reality of his childhood, embodied by figurines
and old trees, nothing less surreal than a movie set, a backdrop
somewhere a city pulses like an artery, full of heat
some created thing. he steals a cigarette
from his mother's purse, retreating to the back porch
somewhere a boy dreams of kissing the football star, square
on the mouth
with only a tin pan of cat food and an eternity
of dumb, unmovable stars to stare at.

inside, the siblings sleep in their rooms, dreaming
of new cars and top 40 radio, the mother warms
somewhere kids are fucking on country roads, listening to heavy
metal, hiding beer in their glove boxes
the kitchen, turns on the oven, busy in the act
of making something out of nothing. he smokes
somewhere old classmates are making their parents happy,
enjoying a life full of sport utility vehicles and endless, beautiful
babies
on the porch, the house behind him a thing
perpetually burning, and suddenly he is 14, sneaking out
somewhere people are doing what they really want
with no place to go, imagining a thing bigger
than this dirt and one tree—a world that moves
somewhere there is something more faithful than television
and is knowable, a place not teetering
on the edge of collapse.

so, he comes back to this spot, pulled
by an innate need to fix things
somewhere people don't secretly fantasize about death
that stay broken, to be the good son,
the good brother, the good person, again
somewhere religion isn't a substitute for thinking
again and again, confident
in the knowledge that he cannot save them
somewhere people are being forgiven
from burning houses, tornadoes, divorces, propane bills
or the ceaselessness of struggle, the blow, the head-on
collision that has become their collective lives.

so, they wave from the house, the props are all left in place
as he drives down brown gravel to the spot
somewhere people leave and don't look back
where dirt gives way to asphalt, highway
interstate—something far away from canyons of
somewhere someone isn't compelled to make sense of it in a poem
red dirt and the violence of lifelong despair,
a place where he forgets about solution and resolution, his mind always
preoccupied by the unlimited possibilities of failure.
somewhere the world is not like this

on collaging childhood photographs

they're much easier to deal with this way, mummified
in tissue shrouds and acrylic medium, half-hidden
by paint and wax, insulated by newsprint, held back
by tar and elmers glue, gagged with corrugated cardboard
i can control them like this, layers of glaze
and found textures becoming a bullwhip
in the center ring—back! back! junior high school pictures!
down birthday party! down christmas 1985!
i can stick my head in the mouth of wedding shots, neatly
blotting out the parts where the skull is crushed
by the strong jaws of bad perms and trailer house lighting
even the toughest shetland pony pics and years
of wood-paneled backdrops can be tamed with
spray mount, x-acto knives, and oil pastel

the face of things is often revealed in something covered,
willfully obscured, juxtaposed, scratched out and erased
the images of fishing trips gone wrong, absentee parents,
pictures of bunny slippered feet and forced smiles,
will only confess when forced, slapped with scissors
and scotch tape, clogged together with years of magazine ads,
baked bean wrappers, bits of roadmap, and faces
blanked into silent ovals, their reality teased
and fucked into the truth, a thing that always must be coaxed
from beneath limitless, impermeable layers

having never succeeded as a chain smoker

i've failed to uphold it, to carry the torch
lit somewhere with a burning match at the bottom
of the family tree. i've seen them all
smoldering, brooding, waving them like a wand
over the contents of their conversations,
ceremonial smoke that crosses generations
of emphysema and wheezing asthmatics
with snap-closing cig pouches stuffed into
oversized purses

"good that you never even started" grandma says
looking for matches, unlit cigarette bobbing and weaving
from the edge of her lip. "no need to feel left out yet though"
she ignites, the classic dramatic smoking pause
and slow exhale, "there's always the chance
that you might still marry and get divorced."

the grandparents

so undisturbed they might as well have been nothing more
than hillbilly salt and pepper shakers, bought probably
for too much money at dogpatch usa, dollywood
or any gift shop in branson, and it's as if they live on a shelf
surrounded by theme parks represented in china
plates and an enameled cedar plaque which reads
      if momma says no, just ask grandma
i'm warmed by the idea of family hee-haw,
that i could come from those who would buy their own likeness
in tableware, those whose only advice for me when leaving is:
      it's really all about the right gun, or like squirrel hunting
      you make the wrong choice and all you have left
      is one front foot and a little piece of tail

misplaced

it is that absolute flatness, the stillness of a landscape
made of red dirt and farm machinery
that made me waste my childhood
brooding in a room with fake wood paneling
covered with magazine clippings
and scotch tape

i realize this as i speed across wide stretches of
barren highway at 2am,
moving towards an invisible night horizon
across a world that seems almost lunar
in its strangeness

after another wasted night of smoky bars and poverty
jet set, i creep home again, eager to beat the sun
i slide past the same faded billboards
and trash-filled canyons i cursed in adolescence

oil rig beacons in the distance reflect off my window like
a remembered winter—white flash and blur, reminiscent
of days spent staring out the window of a cracker box
skirted with tin
looking at endless empty fields, frozen and dusted
planes of snow full of sleeping wheat
and me at the window, lost
in a midwestern siberia with no trees

at night, this nothing draws me home, pulling
at things inside me that no amount
of substance abuse or poisoned thought can kill
behind the wheel in the dark
i am 14 on the back porch
smoking stolen cigarettes, staring
at skies that look like impossible painted movie sets

elegy for a cousin who has fallen off the face of the planet

i remember your red bangs, jacked up
impossibly tall and impermeable to oklahoma weather and
sisterly catfights, a smart mouth and heavy
metal lps thumb-tacked to pink bedroom walls
chippendales calendars and an eternity of cheap lipstick
to my elementary school brain, you were cool as shit
playing the flute and smoking shoplifted cigarettes
sneaking in to see "porky's revenge" 3 times with
a pack of big haired girlfriends

on summer nights we slept on air mattresses that smelled
of lake water and spilled orange soda, surrounded
by TG&Y box fans stuffed into every open window and
you dared me to do the unthinkable
          eat 3 pieces of cat food, slowly
          and i'll tell you something good
rewarding me with stories of your elaborately plotted future
a marriage to a corey haim look-alike who would gladly
pay your way through veterinary school and place you
in a house full of exotic birds and black leather furniture
big enough to blot out any memories
of used station wagons, sno-kone stands
or the coffee cup cafe
          unicorns can be scientifically engineered
          i know this

those times when you tolerated me in your bedroom
listening to you and your girlfriends talk, i attached myself
to the corner, silently dying to hear and remember everything
knowing there could be nothing more amazing than to be a
trash-mouthed high school bad girl
having furtive sex with beefy auto-body repair students
from the el reno junior college, never studying and still making As
telling teachers, coaches, parents, and convenience store workers to

kiss my ass, baby
i don't need this small town cheerleader
bull shit

i thought surely you'd be the first to escape

but you are not here now
moved quietly in a wrecked ford escort from one map dot
to another, supporting a vo-tech dropout who runs from work
as if it were sex or love and has forgotten
that you are pretty and sweet

when i see you now at funerals and weddings
your eyes are those of someone perpetually dozing
lulled from years of struggle and domestic boredom
i try shaking you awake with questions that remind me
that i am rude and sanctimonious, separated from you
by time and age and fashion and radio formats and
designer shoes
        so, are you happy?
        is this how you thought things might be?

        oh, i have my babies now.
and there they are, loud and fire-headed
hanna-barbera versions of you, clinging
to your legs, looking at me much like you do
a person they hardly know
a cousin who understands nothing

what is left

at first, it's as if she is on fire
in my car. a rawness, a heat
that sits too close, telling me things
i have no right or desire to hear, a privilege
granted me for simply being present
this is before i know
that it is more than just her personality
i'm not attracted to, a neediness, eyes
that stay on me, the warmth of something
that, even in the expanse of my old car, can always
find a way to be too close

you can't look at these, she warns
after i don't ask to, shuffling a shoebox
in her lap, full of what must have been
an early version of her, unicorned diary
entries, the loopy handwriting of elementary
love sickness, heart-dotted, pink entries
held in for years by miniature padlocks,
things broken open, i imagine, with small
painted fingernails, butter knives, the roundness
of safety scissors, secrets cracked open later
after all the tiny keys have been lost

once there, we are not unlike a couple in love
walking between jungle gyms and barbecue grills,
which perch like one-legged birds at the edges
dotting the perimeter of grass
and sidewalk, and she walks ahead of me, heavy
with lighter fluid and piles of school photos, the evidence
of someone she—elfin hippy,
unwashed hair and sleepy-stoned-eyes—now scarcely
resembles, a younger twin, a cheerleader,
a valentine, something to be burned
beyond all recognition

in the distance golfers ignore us, i stand back
as she fills the empty grill with the contents
of her childhood, spilled in the shapes of class
notes, friendship bracelets, legal documents
with curled edges and blurred print,
a damaged girlhood wrenched into a wisp
of smoke, a streak in the air

photos curl in the fire, turn black
disappear and for the first time,
her eyes are elsewhere, focused
on a point i can't see, we are alone now
i don't want to remember this
she says, and i wonder exactly what this is,
exactly what i am seeing

and later we might talk about this, why things like this
must be burned, the cruelness of remembering everything
and how, once gone, these things became
even more real, ghostly in their potency,
more present than not, conspicuous
in their absence

but at that moment there is only sky and grass and a bit of smoke
she says little and i stay quiet
a scattering of blackness flakes into the breeze
as we walk back to my car, hair smelling of it
            funny, i really don't feel any better
she says, eyes wet
and i agree, imagining the warm ashes
as we sit in my car at the edge of a green we will never see again
surrendering slowly to the still of manicured golf grass, giving way
almost imperceptibly to dark rolling hills of wheat

my father, one of those things i never write about

it is one of those things i keep thinking i'll figure out
when i'm older—along with computers, investment programs
and religion. it is a nagging, a leaking
faucet that will eventually ruin everything
under the kitchen sink

it comes back in the shape of my own body, curved
posture and slender fingers, my face
when i've been sick with worry for days, madly
unshaven, it rests on me constantly—a presence
over my head, a quietness with my name
attached, an irrational anger that comes like
a gunshot in the face, a thrown fit

it is the arch of a half-built church, a stoned
precision, a neatness fallen accidentally
out of disaster. and it is the wrench of lumber
and dirt, things forced into being
a shape that draws
my eyes away from the road after the light turns green
and i still haven't moved

my fears that i am a bad person are once again confirmed

when you call with your good news, your voice turning
the cushions on my couch into the plastic
multi-colored seating of high school, back when i was
gangly and 15 and while even a year younger,
you were already swiss-engineered in your
adjustment, primed
for a life of perfect relationships and houses and poems
and educations in europe, leaving me
missing you and secretly hoping
for your failure

the cat leaves the room as i spit out "that's great"
a wet hairball of resentment, feeling it
like a lump under my skin or newly rediscovered third nipple
some appendage i forgot that i had, happy
that the lights are turned off and i don't get to see
myself reflected in living room windows, the involuntary
eye-rolling when i say it, your voice and my pettiness
momentarily drowned out by my quiet apartment,
the dusty click of my wheels spinning

ties

i lie in what has become my sister's bedroom—horses
and unicorns dominating every flat surface and nail polish
lined up aggressively on shelves that once held the books
i never had time to read
and i remember

that there were some car seats that couldn't be fixed
spring-riddled and mouse chewed, gracefully removed
from 56 chevies and galaxy 500s those were
the ones my great-grandfather would sacrifice to
the junk pile, to later be rescued by my young mother
for use as tree house couches, tied to the branches
of pear trees with baling wire and twine.

and there she would eat too-green pears with her sister
until they were nauseous and wasp-stung, sometimes
falling and twisting the ankles of their pixie-stick legs
and the grandmother woman who kept them
would force them to cut their happiness down out of fear
that the wind would rain down rotten car seats like
judgment from god

by age 4 i am under the same tree and my mother
is trapped blocks away, selling pickled eggs and beer
to oil field workers as i disappear in the remains of
a car lot, rusted frames frozen to the ground like
locust husks, home to bee hives and stray cats

my great-grandfather is wrapped up
and emphysemic in a bed, surrounded by junk
furniture and hillbilly salt and pepper shakers
water coolers and scorpions
from his bed coming a voice thin
as bible pages
            don't you yell at that boy for nothing
            you let him ride his bike in the house
            if he wants to

and i was always hiding
in the carport where she hanged whole
peanut plants to dry like animal carcasses
or under that tree, broad and limitless
as television, painting dried gourds the perfect
shade of powder blue and hanging them in
the lowest branches with strips of stolen quilt rag

in my sister's bed 20 years later i count the hundreds of glowing
stars arranged across the ceiling, disappointed
that they are brighter and more interesting
than those outside the house
i wonder if in her own room, my mother remembers
car seats and cast iron bathtubs full of stagnant rainwater
and fights the urge to get in the car at 4am and drive back there
across train tracks where
i left pennies to be smashed thin
by western pacific boxcars

back to that tree under which
sheepdogs and old toys are buried
needing to look up through the branches
and search out the spot where we meet
tied together with wire and rags, a place high enough
to see past the debris slides in which
our childhoods eventually leave us.

III. what happens now

. . . the battle cry of those who are remaking sexuality, remaking our perceptions. A battle cry and a slap in the face of rigid liberalism, of those who refuse to acknowledge the body, sex and death.
—Kathy Acker, *Bodies of Work*

To speak of ourselves—while living in a country that considers us or our thoughts taboo—is to shake the boundaries of the illusion of the ONE-TRIBE NATION.
—David Wojnarowicz, *Close to the Knives*

dear diary

you must love me
you must listen
you must, with the open arms of a mother, a lover, anyone
who has been separated from that which completes them, embrace
the words i put onto the page, absolving me
for the horror that is my life. you must
be grateful, for my generous offering of incendiary honesty, a thing
so intense and blinding that the pen smokes in my hand
as i confess to you what i've seen, what i know, the fantastical chain
of tragedy and chaos and flaring beauty that i carve, using only
my fingernails and keen eye for observational detail,
from the black granite which lays at the innermost core of my soul
and that i then offer up to a frozen, indifferent world—a siberia
of intellectual snobbery that refuses to celebrate the beauty
of chronicled emotion, the austere luster of the truth. my truth.
but you must listen.
you must love me, your paper and my pen meeting on that grand
plane of universality in which all joys are shared and no pain
goes unnoticed, no life uncelebrated, no words
left unread for no one to marvel over in the same way the ancients
marveled over the heavens or the taming of fire

telling

there is a kind of silence just before and after
the saying of it, a pause smothered
in the weight of what happens next, an airless
room of expectation waiting for grief or rage or loss or nothing
to rush in and fill it

        please
mom   lover   honey baby   father   dearest
        listen
i love you   i'm sorry   i don't love you
anymore   i did it   i'm married   i want you
i want a divorce   i hate you   it's yours
i'm gay   i'm straight   i'm so
sorry   i'm positive   i'm negative   i don't know
i lost it   i spent it
i wrecked it   i missed my
period   it's over
they're gone

and then the quiet nausea of fallout, lifetimes
compressed into crawling nanoseconds of
now whats and say somethings and looks
on faces that refuse to say where they've gone
or when they're coming back
and then there's you
trying to remember what a different place the world was
just a few moments before

missed

all is fucked up that ends
fucked up, he begins—telling me
that he misses it every day and hates himself
for thinking of it lovingly as a needle
pumps him full of B-12 in the sterile cloud
of a methadone clinic examining room, savoring
the sharp lick of hypodermic, the flushing
whir of memory it produces, a warm rush
of sickness with shot after shot after shot after shot
and even the doctor's voice nods off
in the face of it
          you look like you've been hit by a train
and i'm so fucked up and i still miss it
          you have those junkie teeth now
and even then i miss it

suspension of disbelief

it's exhausting pretending these dinosaurs are real, accepting
that volcanoes can happen in our back yards, watching bruce willis throw
himself out of skyscraper windows and allowing him to live. it's tiring
believing in the possibility of identical cousins and bionic women
with perfectly feathered hair, but we must do it

it's a skill best learned early in life, whether it's on the wooden pew
of a country church or in front of a rabbit-eared zenith, sometimes
you have to let yourself be duped, feigning belief
without actually believing, pretending

that they actually will call you tomorrow, that things can't really get any worse,
that the tedium of daily life is more than a carefully orchestrated dance,
designed, choreographed, and computer enhanced to distract us
from the ground we stand on, from the few things in life we think are real

like a hole in the head

i heard it in the sound of a power drill, embracing
the skull of a young woman, radiant
a "beautiful poem" written in blood, bone
and cranial fluid on the white tiles
of her bathroom floor

i still fight the urge to write them
in my head, the held lines
heavier than speech and symbolism
verse that can be spoken
only by the round, swollen mouth
of the forehead, no bigger than a drinking straw
a common writing utensil

     gravity is the enemy. the adult
     is its victim. society is its disease
     trepanation is the cure
they say enhanced cranial physiology is easy
it takes only 30 minutes to cross the barrier
of your own skull, so i listen
to the blood in my head, the pulse

of those who journey
with corkscrews and 7mm drill bits
pushing them through bathrooms and
partially sterilized garages to find it—
     a buoyancy, an incoming tide
     a rush of blood and enlightenment
     a silence for the first time in years

     and you are drilling away, and there is
     a paranoia thinking you won't know when
     you've gotten through. and then suddenly
     you can stop
     when there is no more resistance

the gift

people should know when they are trying to kill you
whether it's with a gun or a dick
a knife or silence, a fist
or years of practiced indifference and second-hand
smoke, the slow, smothering weight
of wasted time
it doesn't matter how they do it
as long as they know

that it's a gift they give you, an efficient killing
a murder with intent, finishing quickly before
discovering it years later at the table
forks held like weapons, everyone suddenly knowing
what should have been done years before

six degrees of the devil

yes, literally, everything is the devil. everything
you do means that you could be / are / might / should
go to hell. directly to hell. everything weird is "new age"
and "new age" is the devil. everything we see / touch / think / hear
is infused with subliminal evil, and all evil is the work of the devil.
television is the devil. rock music is, obviously, the devil.
(as are those who listen to / play / condone it) all things "occult"
are the devil. "the exorcist," while being about the devil, is actually
the devil. rated "R" is the devil. not going to church is the devil.
halloween is the devil. ouija boards are the devil, as is talking / thinking
about them. hypnotism is the devil. your dreams may be the devil,
and probably are. your body is the devil, or at the very least
his playground. and you, yourself, while you might not even know it
could be the devil. and then there is the devil himself
who is, well . . . the devil.

cadaver poem

first i would have to name it, probably "patrice"
regardless of anatomy, it would have the name
i was never allowed to bestow on cats or other
lesser childhood pets and it wouldn't mind

and before i could cut and dismantle delicate
folds of lung or muscle, i'd first examine
scars, the evidence of a life lived, and fill in
the necessary details: the obvious remnants
of a stray dog bite, appendicitis, the aftermath
of college car accident, the curved pink
reflection of a backyard tree fall,
forgotten proof of blood brotherhood
the faded india of a lover's pet name

i would have to give it a life out of air
before i could disassemble it, consider it
unfeeling meat, specimen. i would mourn
the slack face and empty, stitched skull,
look deep into emptied sockets before wrenching
free the heart with my hands and wondering
who might have broken this cold, ugly muscle?
who might have filled it?

sometimes it happens

like this, you are driving home
down a street you can maneuver like your own bedroom
in the dark, flavored chain store coffee banging against
the walls of your stomach as you turn up the radio
and hear it
trickling tinnily from the blown out rear speakers, covering
every inch of the interior, clinging to every faded piece of plastic molding,
soaking every inch of gray carpeting, coating
your ears with the saccharine sound of the beach boys
        . . . *don't worry baby*

and you hear it and suddenly know that brian wilson
predicted your soul, sitting bearded, fat, and crazy
at a piano writing a song perfectly suited for fuzzed out
speakers and solitary night drives down slicked roads
in your mother's hand-me-down oldsmobile

so your only option is to pull into the parking lot of a dunkin donuts
and cry the slow, heaving sobs that come along
to remind you that there is more in your chest than bone
and blood and empty pockets of air
        . . . *everything's gonna work out alright*

you grip the wheel and choke on the beauty of that sweet, necessary
lie and the reality of your own empty apartment with
no one there to tell it

this poem is haunted

we spend most of our lives this way, governed
by the rules of avoidance. narrowly scraping past
unavoidable pains, folding up the quilts
we can't sleep under any more, listening
for the rattling of chains, waiting for the things we break
to come back to us—the underwater sounds
of those we have drowned, whose faces
it might have been better to never have loved.

retained

i was so glad when you died
i sobbed with guilt for an hour
in my tiny kitchen, wringing
a dishtowel in your honor

we could all grieve publicly then
forgetting the long lapses
between visits, the moments
when you cursed and forgot
names, refusing to become
a martyr for your illness

it was more a wedding than a memorial, too many flowers
and dry cake, all of us
drinking cocktails and
listening to your favorite
dionne warwick albums, reveling
in the exquisite tragedy of it all

i wonder what your midwestern
parents must think of us, flippant
desensitized queens speaking
too loudly about your disease
as if it were a bad haircut, or
an unwanted party guest who had
just stepped out of the room

twice i find myself standing alone
near your casket, a sleek burial bullet
which compels me to re-evaluate my
entire sexual history on the spot
each burst of intimacy becoming
a brush with hypodermic fire, roulette
with body fluids
i imagine a sleeping demon resting
inside me, waiting to spring forth

disguised as a bacterial infection,
respiratory failure, or eggplant colored
blotches pushing out from
beneath the skin

in your absence came a guilt i hadn't felt
in years, and the memory of sunday school
teachers discussing punishment, perversion,
and deviancy before i even knew
i was one

i struggle to remember the paint
you never cleaned out from under your
nails, or the painting you stored in my
apartment for over a year—large, awkward,
half-finished
but too often, this image is smothered
by what you became, a caged thing
bound with intravenous tubing and
untouched food trays. a skeleton
kept warm with hospital blankets
and protease cocktails

now that everything else has left
it's your eyes that i have kept with me
wild and knowing in the end, with a look that said
i will not let you forget
i will live inside you

figuring out what sex means

fuck movies tell us nothing about sex
or love, but everything about consumption
i never learned anything from spontaneous locker room
orgies or straight auto mechanics who decide to really
"fix" the frat boys car, i never saw myself in the faces
of shaved and oiled ken dolls emerging
from santa monica swimming pools with blow
dried hair to have the kind of sex in which condoms mysteriously
appear and no one stops to talk about it
i never learned anything about the redemptive
and healing powers of soul-wrenching, all-encompassing
love from power tool, hot boys of the barrio or five hours of
nutts and butts

i realize this at some point in the am, hiding
in a cubicle of a 24-hour adult video emporium,
my car having delivered me here after a short
eternity of driving the streets of a town that refuses
to be familiar

they don't even look at you when you come in
surrounded by all manner of rubber genitalia
and packaged carnality, i don't matter
and can vanish easily next to a black dildo,
bigger than a grown man's arm

there is something secure about this—
a rented booth with a lock on the door
like the wool-warmth of a sweater pulled
over your head, a few seconds
of disorienting, comforting dark.
the safe anonymity of a folding chair,
and a tv screen

i keep thinking that i'll find it here.
maybe in the mechanized, ritual onscreen
robot fucking or the shuffling sounds of strangers
in nearby booths. i can look for clues shot across
Plexiglas screens or dropped on the floor,
scattered among half-smoked cigarettes
and empty bottles of mr. wonderful poppers

you can sit on a creaking metal chair and wait
forever, feeding dollar bills into a machine
and thinking that something should make sense,
hoping that some light of realization will
suddenly click on, bright enough to burn out
the retinas of your eyes.
biding time until that moment of red-eared heat comes
that car-sick moment when the reality of our lives
becomes suddenly clear, when the money runs out
and the foreign and familiar sound of sex
shuts off, when someone says that thing
that maybe
you've been waiting years to hear.

fear of flying

1.

white knuckled, you are
afraid of what happens next
the calming flight attendant gone, pushed
against your seat by something
heavier than your lap belt
you suddenly come to know
when the wheels are no longer
touching the ground

2.

grandma wanda flies to colorado
at 57, after years of calling
everyone crazy, badmouthing them
as "flying death buses," she bites
the bullet, surprising everyone
with a trip to the mountains
it's not so bad she will say
except for the no smoking thing
later i hear her whistling
leaving on a jet plane, in her tiny kitchen

3.

i love you far too much
to actually be with you, he says
after the sun has burned off
whatever drugs are left in our bodies
if we fucked this up, i know
we'd never survive it
a jet passes over the apartment complex, deafening
and the threat of what is at risk
makes the forfeiture of our happiness
seem small

4.
she designed in-flight magazines for a living
her primary goal to distract people
from the fact that they could plummet, a fiery ball
of metal and skin, to their deaths at any given second
it's easy, she laughs
just provide lots of expensive advertising

5.
it takes nine hours to get there
most of it flying over ocean that eventually
becomes only a shade, relentless
as the 12 year-old twitch beside me
my dad is a pilot, and he says all the time
that the world would shut down without its wings
i nod, again, again, and think of the man
who waits for me on on the island, who doesn't love me
at all, but is happy to see me land there
with only water in any given direction

6.
having never left the state of oklahoma, my sister
questions me about them, *what is it like?*
i explain seats, smoking lights, minuscule
airplane food. *rich people fly*
she pauses, *and if i could, i'd fly everywhere—*
mainly australia. just as our local crop duster
mists our house with poison.

7.

for my 15th christmas, my father flies
me to see him. at 30 minutes, the trip
allows for just one soda before straightening
our seats and landing. as is my luck, i sit
by the most horrified man in the world, sweaty
and only barely contained in his seat.
but what, i ask, *do you know about airplanes?*
i know enough, he whispers, *about the world
to be afraid.*

saved from drowning

it is summer when we fuck
for the first and only time
in my car you are sinister and
soft spoken, almost edible
james dean vulnerability with
a silence that can pass for kindness
or intelligence in some people
"i wouldn't normally do this"
you say twice

and next you are on your mother's
floral couch, distanced—arms crossed
telling your story, pulling bits of it out
slowly as surgical needles
a high school affair with the star
quarterback, clandestine attachment
from 8th grade and beyond, ending
with graduation and abandonment
the quarterback retreating into white-trash
hetero domesticity with some knocked-up
cheerleader and a silver trailer house

you tell it like an after-school special
gone to hell, full of secret sex
on muddy roads in farm trucks and
camaros wrapped around trees
revenge with no happy queer prom
or public service announcement
for an ending

i choke on the urge to laugh
when i look at you, a trinity of
senior pictures poised symmetrically
above your head, all american boy
with car, with baseball uniform
smiling with mom and dad
you are balled into the corner of
the couch, eyes suddenly beestung
with the telling of it, your body
stark as a skyscraper
towering above the gun racks
in the hallway, the i luv country
bathmats and massey-fergusson
parked against the backdoor

it's a cinder block in my stomach
when i drive home, waiting
to see you years later
drowned in a bar, eyes dark and lungs
full from years of submersion
in anonymous car sex
generic genitals with no last name
i'm happy for your story, the memory
of your face
grateful to have been pulled
from the water

this is where i know you from

his face is what comes
as we lay twisted together on an overstuffed couch
lit ridiculously by cable television and subdued
track lighting. and while it's partially hidden by shadow,
the blur of your face becomes one i knew at 16
after i meet you in a bar, a blunt
cut marine who asks repeatedly
if he can kiss me, and never
for my name

with the solid weight of you over me
you are a million men, crammed
into pockets of badly lit cigarette smoke, perched
on barstools with gin and tonics, repeating
        yes, yes, yes, with all the fucking
        parade marching and glossy magazines
        and fucking "my best friend's weddings"
        in the world, and this is still the best
        we can do, we are still reduced
        to this?
and so i'm glad i can't always see your face
a plate of glass, a badly staked tent

across the room the television flickers, an animal
drags its kill into the woods and you breathe
into my neck, i wonder how it might feel different
if i were someone you cared for, or you
a thing i really wanted, something more
than an available warmth
that keeps his eyes closed

the project of the poem

for Albert Goldbarth

this poem is about being poor, full
of images of midwestern poverty
and intolerance, it sings of being shot
out into the world to make good
and its story is really nothing new

this poem is about the women
inhabiting my life--the mother
sister grandmother friend and
fag hag, all of them sisters
in my mind, a single
wondrous thing

this poem like too many others
is about my childhood, saturated
with farm animals, divorce
and cigarette smoke, it begins
where it end and finds the speaker
standing always at the same spot

this poem is the halfway house
for other destitute poems with no place to go

this poem is about everything
everything everything everything
and everything

this poem is about nostalgia for a childhood that never existed

this poem carries the weight of a family history
on its back, with no time, no energy and no
breath for the voice to tell it

this poem is about craziness and how it becomes
normal, and the man in taco tico, repeating
the japanese do not have a future tense
the japanese cannot predict the future
and i may die tomorrow

this poem is so dirty that no pen is willing
to write its nasty name

this poem is about hardship, about my student
who, after weeks of fading out, vanishes
materializing weeks later at my office door,
black-eyed with a chicken scratched essay
in her hand. "i live in my car now"
she says, disappearing again
this time for good

this poem is about disaster and trailer houses
the inability to save those you love
from the reality of their lives

this poem too
is about loss, the kind
that could be avoided but isn't
and it mentions the woman who
inadvertently tossed her baby over
niagara falls, it reminds me to stop
and remember everything i've stupidly
thrown away

this poem is about the first boy i ever loved, a fresh-faced
inhabitant of walnut grove who I watched every week
and whose adolescent image haunts my sleep in reruns

this poem is about breaking things
it centers around fit-throwing and suddenly
becoming your father

this poem is about moving, flat tires, u-hauls
gas stations and alien roads, carrying
your world on your back

this poem is about landscape, pushed
flat and scraped severe
by the cosmic putty knife, it contains
the serenity of rolling hills, the shudder
of suddenly knowing you are alone

this poem, if you can stomach it
is about fags, and being one
its about name calling, the air outside
bars at 2am, the shocking knowledge
that you are hated

this poem is about my mother, the brushing back
of her hair, it strives to understand
the way the subtle behaviors of those we love
are imprinted on us, pillow lines
on freshly awakened faces

this poem is about fucking
not making love or having sex
but something more consumptive, fucking
and fucking and fucking

this poem is about the baby who was carried away
by a tornado, found unharmed and crying in a field of dirt
screaming out in squawking baby-speak just what he'd seen

this poem, sadly
is about nothing

this poem is about memory and tupperware
the green plastic colander my grandmother melted
in our new dishwasher, and the aluminum cone
used to mash out berries for canning,
and the mush left at the bottom that tells the tale

this poem is about mild insanity and obsessive
house cleaning, it is full of ammonia-based detergents
and manic despair, the inability to save yourself
from the reality of your own life

this poem is about every boy i ever wanted
that didn't want me back, it centers around heat,
suffocation, wanting and all other forms
of delicious agony

this poem shouldn't even be read
or remembered

and this poem tries hard
to say too much,
that our stories are all interchangeable
that we all, despite the sad or wonderful
exceptionality of our lives,
become archetypes of a sort, lego blocks of humanity
all of us full of the great themes
        love and tragedy and loss and
        beautiful stinging joy